WITNESS TO HISTORY

MAJOR CULTURAL MOVEMENTS

Inside the

WOMEN'S RIGHTS MOVEMENT

 Gareth Stevens
PUBLISHING

By Jill Keppeler

Please visit our website, www.garethstevens.com. For a free color catalog of all our high-quality books, call toll free 1-800-542-2595 or fax 1-877-542-2596.

Cataloging-in-Publication Data

Names: Keppeler, Jill.
Title: Inside the Women's Rights Movement / Jill Keppeler.
Description: New York : Gareth Stevens Publishing, 2018. | Series: Eyewitness to history: major cultural movements | Includes index.
Identifiers: LCCN ISBN 9781538211694 (pbk.) | ISBN 9781538211717 (library bound) | ISBN 9781538211700 (6 pack)
Subjects: LCSH: Women's rights–United States–History–Juvenile literature. | Feminism–History–Juvenile literature.
Classification: LCC HQ1155.K47 2018 | DDC 305.42'0973–dc23

First Edition

Published in 2018 by
Gareth Stevens Publishing
111 East 14th Street, Suite 349
New York, NY 10003

Copyright © 2018 Gareth Stevens Publishing

Designer: Katelyn E. Reynolds
Editor: Therese Shea

Photo credits: Cover, pp. 1 (person), 19 (bottom), 21 (top), 23 (Steinem) Bettmann/ Getty Images; cover, p. 1 (background image) George Rinhart/Corbis via Getty Images; cover, p. 1 (logo quill icon) Seamartini Graphics Media/Shutterstock.com; cover, p. 1 (logo stamp) YasnaTen/Shutterstock.com; cover, p. 1 (color grunge frame) DmitryPrudnichenko/ Shutterstock.com; cover, pp. 1–32 (paper background) Nella/Shutterstock.com; cover, pp. 1–32 (decorative elements) Ozerina Anna/Shutterstock.com; pp. 1–32 (wood texture) Reinhold Leitner/Shutterstock.com; pp. 1–32 (open book background) Elena Schweitzer/ Shutterstock.com; pp. 1–32 (bookmark) Robert Adrian Hillman/Shutterstock.com; p. 5 EMMANUEL DUNAND/AFP/Getty Images; p. 7 (top) National Portrait Gallery/ Wikipedia.org; p. 7 (bottom) Smithonian National Portrait Gallery/Wikipedia.org; pp. 9, 15 Universal History Archive/UIG via Getty Images; pp. 11, 13 (top) courtesy of the Library of Congress; p. 13 (bottom) Everett Historical/Shutterstock.com; p. 17 Lynn Gilbert/Wikipedia.org; p. 19 (top) Carolina Digital Library and Archives. "Murray, Pauli, 1910-1985." 5 July 2007. Online image. UNC University Library. Accessed 8 April 2011/Wikipedia.org; p. 21 (bottom) Anthony Calvacca/New York Post/Photo Archives, LLC via Getty Images; p. 23 (Chisholm) Pictorial Parade/Getty Images; p. 23 (Abzug) Leonard Mccombe/The LIFE Picture Collection/Getty Images; p. 25 (map) Hedgefighter/ Wikipedia.org; p. 25 (image) Barbara Freeman/Getty Images; p. 27 Hulton Archive/ Getty Images.

Printed in the United States of America

CPSIA compliance information: Batch #CW18GS: For further information contact Gareth Stevens, New York, New York at 1-800-542-2595.

CONTENTS

*Words in the glossary appear in **bold** type the first time they are used in the text.*

FIGHTING
for Equality

In 2016, Hillary Clinton became the first woman to accept a major political party's nomination for president of the United States. *"Standing here as my mother's daughter, and my daughter's mother, I'm so happy this day has come,"* she said during her acceptance speech at the Democratic National **Convention**. *"When any barrier falls in America, for anyone, it clears the way for everyone. When there are no ceilings, the sky's the limit."*

Women make up about half the population of the United States, but they've been fighting for equal rights since the founding of the country—and before! Today, the fight continues.

On September 5, 1995, then First Lady of the United States Hillary Clinton spoke at the United Nations Fourth World Conference on Women in Beijing, China. *"If there is one message that echoes forth from this conference,"* she told the crowd, *"let it be that human rights are women's rights and women's rights are human rights, once and for all. Let us not forget that among those rights are the right to speak freely—and the right to be heard."* Women throughout history have sought to exercise these rights.

MORE TO KNOW

One hundred years before Clinton accepted the nomination for president, women were still fighting for the right to vote!

Hillary Clinton is pictured here at the UN conference in 1995. She later would become the secretary of state and a presidential candidate.

FIRST STEPS
to Suffrage

In the early days of the British colonies in North America, married women couldn't own property in their own name or have their own money (with very few exceptions). After the colonies became the United States, each of the original 13 states passed laws making sure that women didn't have suffrage, or the right to vote.

Many women were unhappy with this situation. **Activists,** such as Lucretia Mott and Elizabeth Cady Stanton, started banding together to work toward women's rights and suffrage, even though many people opposed them. *"Any great change must expect opposition, because it shakes the very foundation of privilege,"* Mott said in 1853. Mott, Stanton, and others planned the first women's rights convention in Seneca Falls, New York.

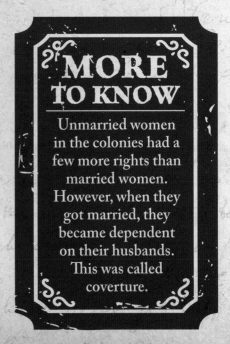

MORE TO KNOW

Unmarried women in the colonies had a few more rights than married women. However, when they got married, they became dependent on their husbands. This was called coverture.

Many of the first women's rights activists were involved in the fight for abolition, or the end to slavery. Mott (below) and Stanton (above) met at an antislavery convention in London, England.

COMMON LAW

The law in the American colonies was based on English common law. According to *Commentaries on the Laws of England* by William Blackstone, "*By marriage, the husband and wife are one person in the law: that is, the very being and legal existence of the woman is suspended during the marriage, or at least is incorporated and consolidated into [made part of] that of her husband.*" According to English law, she stopped being her own person once she married.

SENECA *Falls*

On July 19 and 20, 1848, more than 200 people traveled to Seneca Falls, New York, to take part in the first national meeting of women's rights supporters. On the first day, Elizabeth Cady Stanton read the Declaration of Sentiments, which included these words: *"We hold these truths to be self-evident: that all men and women are created equal."* This sentence echoed the famous phrase in the Declaration of Independence.

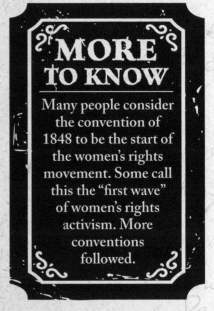

MORE TO KNOW

Many people consider the convention of 1848 to be the start of the women's rights movement. Some call this the "first wave" of women's rights activism. More conventions followed.

The declaration continued, listing many of the ways in which women weren't equal in society. It ended: *"Because women do feel themselves . . . **oppressed**, and . . . **deprived** of their most sacred rights, we insist that they have immediate admission to all the rights and privileges which belong to them as citizens of the United States."*

Before the women's rights convention ended, 100 men and women had signed the Declaration of Sentiments.

THE FIRST CONVENTION

EVER CALLED TO DISCUSS THE

Civil and Political Rights of Women,

SENECA FALLS, N. Y., JULY 19, 20, 1848.

———

WOMAN'S RIGHTS CONVENTION.

———

A Convention to discuss the social, civil, and religious condition and rights of woman will be held in the Wesleyan Chapel, at Seneca Falls, N. Y., on Wednesday and Thursday, the 19th and 20th of July current; commencing at 10 o'clock A. M. During the first day the meeting will be exclusively for women, who are earnestly invited to attend. The public generally are invited to be present on the second day, when Lucretia Mott, of Philadelphia, and other ladies and gentlemen, will address the Convention.*

———

* This call was published in the *Seneca County Courier*, July 14, 1848, without any signatures. The movers of this Convention, who drafted the call, the declaration and resolutions were Elizabeth Cady Stanton, Lucretia Mott, Martha C. Wright, Mary Ann McClintock, and Jane C. Hunt.

A FRIEND OF THE CAUSE

Abolitionist Frederick Douglass was one of the people who signed the Declaration of Sentiments. Douglass was a believer in women's rights and a friend to the movement. In a speech in April 1888 in Washington, DC, he told the crowd that a great truth is *"bound to go on till it becomes the thought of the world. Such a truth is woman's right to equal liberty with man. She was born with it."*

SUSAN B. *Anthony*

A REVOLUTION

Susan B. Anthony was a writer, speaker, and, with Stanton, the publisher of *The Revolution*, a newspaper that supported the women's suffrage movement. In honor of Anthony's 50th birthday, poet Phoebe Cary, who was also an assistant editor at the newspaper, wrote a poem including this verse:
*She, caring not for loss of men,
Nor for the world's confusion,
Has carried on a civil war,
And made a "Revolution."*

Many women worked for women's rights, but Susan B. Anthony was one of the most famous. Anthony, who was born in 1820 in Massachusetts, fought for most of her life for the right to vote. Anthony (and 15 other women) voted illegally in the US presidential election of 1872. Anthony was arrested for it. At her trial, the judge reminded her that she was in court because of the existing laws.

Anthony said in return, *"Yes, but laws made by men, under a government of men, interpreted by men and for the benefit of men. The only chance women have for justice in this country is to violate [break] the law, as I have done, and as I shall continue to do."*

10

MORE TO KNOW

When the Nineteenth Amendment to the US Constitution was approved in 1920, it gave women the right to vote. It was sometimes called the Susan B. Anthony Amendment.

In 1866, Susan B. Anthony (left) and Elizabeth Cady Stanton (right) started the American Equal Rights Association, which later split into the National Woman Suffrage Association and the American Woman Suffrage Association.

CARRIE
Chapman Catt

Anthony, Mott, Stanton, and many other early activists worked very hard to achieve the right to vote. Unfortunately, none of them were ever able to do so legally. As the first suffrage fighters grew older and died, new leaders stepped up to take on the fight.

Carrie Chapman Catt was one of these leaders. Born in 1859 in Wisconsin, she became the president of the National American Woman Suffrage Association in 1900 and then again in 1915, leading it through the approval of the Nineteenth Amendment. In 1921, she spoke to the graduating class at Iowa State College, ending with these words: *"To the wrongs that need resistance, to the right that needs assistance, to the future in the distance, give yourselves."*

MORE TO KNOW

The National American Woman Suffrage Association that Carrie Chapman Catt led was formed by combining the National Woman Suffrage Association and the American Woman Suffrage Association.

Lucretia Mott died in 1880. Elizabeth Cady Stanton followed in 1902, and Susan B. Anthony died 4 years later in 1906. This was still 14 years before women were granted the right to vote. According to the *New York Times*, Anthony told a friend not long before her death, *"To think I have had more than 60 years of hard struggle for a little liberty, and then to die without it seems so cruel."*

Suffragists, or those fighting for suffrage, often marched in parades in support of their cause. As time went on, some even picketed the White House, which means they marched and stood outside with signs.

GETTING *the Vote*

"NOTHING CAN TAKE FROM THEM THEIR TRIUMPH"

US Secretary of State Bainbridge Colby signed the proclamation of the Nineteenth Amendment in private at his home, without any ceremony, photographs, or female witnesses. Some of those who'd fought so hard for the right were upset by this, as they'd hoped to have the moment preserved. *"However,"* suffragist Abby Scott Baker noted in a *New York Times* story, *"the women of America have fought a big fight and nothing can take from them their triumph."*

As the suffragists continued to protest and fight, states gradually started to give women the right to vote. By 1919, women in 18 states or territories had some voting rights. By June 1919, US Congress approved an amendment to the Constitution granting women the right to vote. The Nineteenth Amendment was finally **ratified** on August 18, 1920. It reads: *"The right of citizens of the United States to vote shall not be denied . . . by the United States or by any State on account of sex."*

One big fight for women's rights was over—but there were still many to go. Suffragist Alice Paul said after the ratification, *"It is incredible to me that any woman should consider the fight for full equality won. It has just begun."*

In this photo, Alice Paul and other women celebrate the ratification of the Nineteenth Amendment.

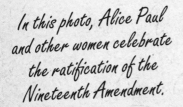

SECOND *Wave*

By the 1960s, women started to seek equality in new areas, beginning the second wave of the women's rights movement. The civil rights movement of the 1950s and 1960s inspired them. Women taking jobs that were once only held by men during and after World War II also helped create a desire for change.

In 1963, journalist Betty Friedan published the book *The Feminine Mystique*. In it, she questioned the belief at that time that women were meant only to marry, have children, and care for homes and men. Friedan wrote, *"As [a wife] made the beds, shopped for groceries, matched slipcover material [for furniture], ate peanut butter sandwiches with her children . . . she was afraid to even ask of herself the silent question—'Is this all?'"*

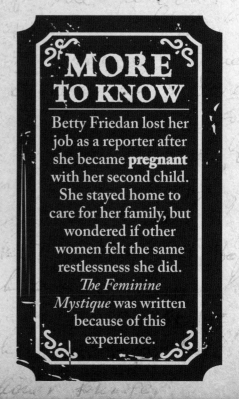

MORE TO KNOW

Betty Friedan lost her job as a reporter after she became **pregnant** with her second child. She stayed home to care for her family, but wondered if other women felt the same restlessness she did. *The Feminine Mystique* was written because of this experience.

Betty Friedan's book quickly sold many copies. It's credited with creating a rise in feminism, or the belief women and men should have equal rights and opportunities.

FEMININE MYSTIQUE

Friedan's phrase *"feminine mystique"* is the assumption that marriage, housework, and raising children alone should satisfy all women. Assuming this meant believing that women didn't need careers, roles in politics, or more than a basic education. Friedan said many women wanted and needed more: *"It was a strange stirring, a sense of dissatisfaction, a **yearning** that women suffered in the middle of the twentieth century in the United States."*

EQUALITY NOW!

PAULI MURRAY

Dr. Pauli Murray was one of the cofounders of NOW. Born in 1910, Murray was a writer, professor, and civil rights attorney. She was also a lesbian, or a woman attracted to other women, during a time when people didn't often speak about such things. In 1977, she wrote, *"If one could characterize [describe] in a single phrase the contribution of black women to America, I think it would be 'survival with **dignity** against incredible odds.'"*

Many women were encouraged by Friedan's book. They wanted to begin working together to gain more rights and opportunities. However, women's rights weren't a major concern for the US government. Even though Title VII of the Civil Rights Act banned sex **discrimination** in jobs, the Equal Employment Opportunity Commission (EEOC) refused to enforce parts of Title VII.

Friedan and others created the National Organization for Women (NOW) in 1966. Friedan served as its president. She wrote its first statement of purpose, which included the words: *"NOW is dedicated to the proposition that women, first and foremost, are human beings, who, like all other people in our society, must have the chance to develop their fullest human **potential**."*

Murray was also part of the Congress of Racial Equality (CORE), an important group that worked for African American rights beginning in the 1940s.

Dr. Kathryn F. Clarenbach, left, and Betty Friedan are shown here at a NOW meeting in 1968.

NOW had a lot of work ahead. Members wanted to fight employment discrimination and make sure women had equal education opportunities, **maternity leave**, and suitable childcare. Some also wanted to fight for the right to **contraception** and abortion, or the medical process to end a pregnancy. This led to divisions in the movement. Activists broke off into groups in order to fight for rights based on their opinions about these issues.

About a year after the founding of NOW, its members wrote a Bill of Rights for Women. They called for Congress to pass a constitutional amendment guaranteeing equal rights for women. Alice Paul had first introduced an amendment like this, called the Equal Rights Amendment (ERA), back in 1923.

MORE TO KNOW

The Redstockings group was considered more radical, or extreme, than NOW. It was founded during the 1960s.

Margaret Sanger

MARGARET SANGER AND BIRTH CONTROL

Birth control is an important issue in the women's rights movement. Many people believe that women should have the right to control their own ability to reproduce. However, this view was, and sometimes still is, controversial, which means it causes disagreement. Margaret Sanger, who worked as a nurse in New York City in the early 1900s, worked to change views and laws about birth control. *"No woman can call herself free who does not control her own body,"* she wrote.

Members of NOW protest at the New York City office of the EEOC in 1967 below. The organization gradually improved its enforcement of Title VII of the Civil Rights Act.

WOMEN CAN THINK as well as TYPE

SEX SEGREGATION IS AS unfair AS RACE SEGREGATION

I didn't GET A JOB THROUGH THE "New York Times"

NEW FACES
in Government

As time went on, new leaders emerged in the women's rights movement—in government. In 1968, Shirley Chisholm became the first African American woman elected to Congress when she won a seat in the House of Representatives. In 1970, Bella Abzug was also elected to a seat in the House. The number of women running for office—and winning—increased. *"Women are becoming aware, as blacks did, that they can have equal treatment if they will fight for it, and they are starting to organize,"* Chisholm wrote.

In 1971, Shirley Chisholm, Bella Abzug, and Betty Friedan, along with activist Gloria Steinem, founded the National Women's Political Caucus. This group still works today to encourage women to seek public office in order to strengthen female voices in government.

Shirley Chisholm, Bella Abzug, and Gloria Steinem were women from different backgrounds who worked together to fight for women's rights.

Chisholm

Abzug

Steinem

HOPE FOR
a New ERA

As women gained more rights and inched closer to equality, NOW turned its focus to passing the Equal Rights Amendment. The main part of the amendment reads: *"Equality of rights under the law shall not be denied or **abridged** by the United States or by any state on account of sex."* It was meant to prevent laws that discriminated against women.

The members of NOW and others fought hard to convince Congress to pass the ERA. Finally, in 1972, the US Senate approved it. Three-fourths of the states needed to ratify the amendment before it could become law. Though 38 states were needed, only 35 ratified it by the 1982 deadline. The ERA hasn't become law, but activists aren't giving up on it. Many continue to push for the amendment today.

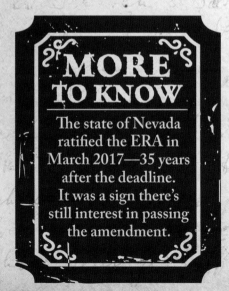

MORE TO KNOW

The state of Nevada ratified the ERA in March 2017—35 years after the deadline. It was a sign there's still interest in passing the amendment.

states ratified (August 2017)
states not ratified (August 2017)

Hawaii was the first state to ratify the ERA. It did so the same day Congress passed the amendment.

A significant milestone for the women's rights movement came on January 22, 1973, when the US Supreme Court ruled on the case *Roe v. Wade.* The court's decision was that women in the United States had a legal right to abortion. *"[Roe v. Wade] has fundamentally altered the legal, medical, and political landscape of this country,"* stated Gloria Feldt, president of Planned Parenthood Federation of America. This decision is still one of the court's most controversial.

THIRD *Wave*

DISCRIMINATION MULTIPLIED

Law professor Kimberlé Crenshaw created the term "intersectionality." She wrote about black women experiencing discrimination based on more than just sex or just race.

"Anti-discrimination law looks at race and gender separately. The consequence of that is when African American women . . . experience either compound or overlapping discrimination, the law initially just was not there to come to their defense . . . Intersectionality was a way of addressing what it was that the courts weren't seeing."

The modern women's rights movement quieted somewhat after the 1970s. However, in the mid-1990s, what some people call the "third wave" of the movement began. Many activists felt the second wave's work was unfinished. And because of the second wave, some women had positions of greater power from which to work for more rights and greater equality.

The first two waves of the women's rights movement were mainly focused on white middle-class or upper-class women. People are still striving to make the women's rights movement more varied and open to everyone. The idea of intersectionality is part of the ideals of the third wave. This means understanding that women of different backgrounds have different challenges to face, so the fight must be for the rights of *all* women.

MORE TO KNOW

Some third wavers dislike the term "feminists" because they think the word excludes men. They want the movement to stress equal rights rather than women's rights.

The third wave of feminism is sometimes credited with the creation of stronger female characters in movies, books, and television. Some of these characters include Mulan in Disney's *Mulan* (1998) and Buffy Summers (played by Sarah Michelle Gellar) in the television show *Buffy the Vampire Slayer* (1997–2003).

THE STRUGGLE
Continues

People disagree about whether the third wave of the women's rights movement continues today. Few disagree that the work must continue. In 2017, despite laws requiring equal pay for men and women, women still earned about 79 cents for every dollar men earned. The Equal Rights Amendment still isn't law. Women are also still underrepresented in politics: only about 19 percent of the members of Congress are female. Women are still fighting for equality at work and in society.

The problems may not be going away, but those who fight them aren't, either. In January 2017, hundreds of thousands of women marched in Washington, DC, and other cities throughout the country and world in support of women's rights. Whatever the future holds, the fight continues.

MORE TO KNOW

In Chicago, Illinois, so many showed up for the women's rights rally that the march was canceled. There was thought to be too many people to walk through the streets safely.

WOMEN'S RIGHTS

THE STRUGGLE THROUGH THE YEARS

1777 — All US states have laws denying women the right to vote.

1848 — The first women's rights convention in the United States takes place in Seneca Falls, New York.

1866 — Elizabeth Cady Stanton and Susan B. Anthony start the American Equal Rights Association.

1869 — The American Equal Rights Association splits into the National Woman Suffrage Association and the American Woman Suffrage Association.

1872 — Susan B. Anthony and other women vote in the presidential election. Anthony is arrested and goes on trial.

1890 — The National Woman Suffrage Association and the American Woman Suffrage Association form the National American Woman Suffrage Association.

1920 — The Nineteenth Amendment is ratified, giving American women the right to vote.

1923 — Alice Paul introduces the Equal Rights Amendment (ERA).

1963 — Betty Friedan publishes the book *The Feminine Mystique*.

1964 — Title VII of the Civil Rights Act bans sex discrimination in the workplace.

1966 — Betty Friedan and others create the National Organization for Women (NOW).

1971 — The National Women's Political Caucus is founded.

1973 — The US Supreme Court rules in favor of abortion in the case *Roe v. Wade*.

1982 — Only 35 of the 38 states needed pass the ERA.

2016 — Hillary Clinton becomes the first woman nominated by a major political party for the office of president.

2017 — Hundreds of thousands of people march for women's rights throughout the United States and the world.

WORDS FROM THE MARCH

Women of all ages took part in the January 2017 marches. Gloria Steinem, by then 82 years old, spoke to marchers in Washington, DC. *"Make sure you introduce yourselves to each other,"* she said, *"and decide what we're going to do tomorrow, and tomorrow and tomorrow. We're never turning back!"* Another speaker at the march in Washington was 6-year-old Sophie Cruz. *"Let's keep together,"* she said, *"and fight for the rights."*

29

GLOSSARY

abridge: to reduce

activist: one who acts strongly in support of or against an issue

contraception: birth control, or things that are done to prevent a pregnancy

convention: a gathering of people who have a common interest or purpose

deprive: to take something away from

dignity: a sense of pride and self-respect

discrimination: unfairly treating people unequally because of their race or beliefs

maternity leave: a period of absence from work granted to a mother before and after the birth of her child

oppress: to treat a person or a group in a way that's unjust or cruel

potential: an ability that can be developed in someone

pregnant: the state of carrying an unborn baby inside the body

ratify: to give formal approval to something

yearning: a wish or desire

FOR MORE
Information

Books

Cooper, Ilene. *A Woman in the House and Senate: How Women Came to the United States Congress, Broke Down Barriers, and Changed the Country.* New York, NY: Abrams Books for Young Readers, 2014.

Fabiny Sarah. *Who Is Gloria Steinem?* New York, NY: Grosset & Dunlap, 2014.

Hollihan, Kerrie Logan. *Rightfully Ours: How Women Won the Vote: 21 Activities.* Chicago, IL: Chicago Review Press, 2012.

Websites

Women's Suffrage
brainpop.com/socialstudies/ushistory/womenssuffrage/
Watch a short movie in which you can learn more about the struggle for suffrage.

Women's Suffrage
ducksters.com/history/civil_rights/womens_suffrage.php
This website offers photos, a quiz, and more information about the fight for the right to vote.

INDEX